ON THE NATURE OF HINGES

TESHELLE COMBS

Teshelle Combs Books

Copyright © 2020 by Teshelle Combs

All Rights reserved, including the rights of reproduction in print or online in any whole or partial form.

Manufactured in the United States of America.

Book layout and design by Nate Combs Media.

ISBN-13: 979-8618689953

Darlings. May we heal.

ON THE NATURE OF HINGES

TESHELLE COMBS

1

Have you ever

Loved someone

Who took the **hinges**

Off the door of your heart?

2

Did they **leave** you

Waiting in your room

With the hallway light

Mocking you?

3

Were you afraid

Time would eat up the **moments**

And they would not come?

4

Were you a f r a i d

Moments would eat up time

And they would

Come back

So different

You wouldn't know

It was them?

5

Did you hide in the bathroom
And let the **lies**
Pick at you
Like crows
In famine?

6

Did the shower curtain
Become your
Only **defense**?

7

Did your **fear**
Drag you by the hair
And let you dry off
On the bath mat?

8

When did you learn

It was safe

To look in

The **mirror**?

9

Where were the people

Who you called **friends**,

And did they know

You'd been calling?

10

When did you

Make yourself leave

The dark of your room

On hands and knees?

11

Had the kitchen   you
Rattling around the drawers
Like there was a point
To you?

missed

12

How many eyes
Did you lie to
When they looked to see
If you were **alright**?

13

When did your

Heart stop beating

Like it was **brea**king

Through its cage?

14

When could you

Chew and swallow

Without **feeling** like

A thief and a beggar?

15

How far did you

Go to make

Sense of the

Light at the **end**

Of the block?

16

When did you

Start to ask

why?

17

When did

Why

Start to **give** you

An answer?

18

When did they
Come back
To **see** how
You were?

19

Did it run

~~Through you~~

Like **cold** knives?

20
Why did **you** let them?

same

same

21
Did they sit
In the **same** old
Chair they used to
And smile?

same

same

same

same

same

same

22

Did you

Smile back

Like you were not

A dead thing?

23

W
i
n
How was the e

And did you

Have too much?

24

When they were

Cross-legged on

Your **bed**,

Did   you

Like   it?

25

How sweetly did

They put their

Arms

Around your frame?

26

Did you shake

When they
Touched your

Cheek

Like they
Did **before**?

27

Did the flutter
Of their **breath**
Make you laugh?

28

When did you

L se yourself?

29
After,

Did you s p r e a d out

On your backs

And make shadow puppets

On the ceiling?

30

Did they look

Like **heaven**

With their

Cheek pressed to

Your pillow?

31

Did you glance at
The clock and **mmrz**
What time their eyes
Drifted closed?

m-m-ri-e

mem-riz

memorize

32

How hard
Did you
pray?

33

Did the coffee

Smell **different**

When they

Made it

In the morning?

34

What was it like

To lean **back**

Against their chest

With nothing else to do?

35

How **<u>sure</u>** were you

When you put the

Door back on the

hinges?

36

How sure were you
The new wasn't **old**
And different wasn't the **same**?

37

Did they
promise?

38

Can

you

recall

what

A promise feels like

When

it

slides

down

your

Throat

like too many pills?

39

Did you **believe** them?

Again

Again

Agrain

Again

Again

40
Again?

Agaen

Again

A gain

Again

Again

Again

Again

Again

Again

A grain

Agiven

Agone

Again

Again

41

When did you

Start to get

comfortable?

42

When did you

Begin preparing for

Dinner and

Quiet nights?

43

Remember when
You **knew** the sound
Of the car engine
Pulling up
And coming to a stop
Around eight
Each night?

44
R-memb-r

That time

It was quarter past

And there was no engine?

45

How did that **last** breath

Squeeze itself out

Without you giving it

permission?

46

How much **silence** passed

With you at the table

Waiting to eat

And watching both plates

Get cold?

47
How did you do it?

48

How did you put your

Feet to the hardwood

And **pull** yourself

To the bathroom?

49

Did it feel like **madness**

To brush your teeth

As if it were a normal night?

50

What did the floor feel like,
Pressed against your ribcage?

51

When the covers
Were over your head,
Did you feel **safe**?

52

Would you

Have given

Anything

For them to

Take the

Door off the

Hinges

One more

time?

53

Did you find a ?

54
Did you **pray** for a note?

55
When did you **stop**

Listening for
The car pulling up
Around eight o'clock?

56

Did you **HATE** them

Real good

And real loud

That one night

You lost it

Because you **lost**

them?

57

Did you **love** them

Real hard

Because they knew you

And you weren't **done**

Learning them?

58

Why do

People

When they

Should

stay?

Leave

64

59
When will they
Come **home**?

60
How long
Does **going**
Take
Someone who is
Long

Gone?

More Works by Teshelle Combs

Let There Be Nine Series

- *Let There Be Nine Vol 1*: **Enneagram Poetry**

- *Let There Be Nine Vol 2*: **Enneagram Poetry**

For Series: Words laced together on behalf of an idea, a place, a world.

- **For Her**
- **For Him**
- **For Them**
- **For Us**

Love Bad Series: Poems About Love. Not Love Poems.

- **Love Bad**
- **Love Bad More**
- **Love Bad Best**

Standalone Poetry Books:

Breath Like Glass

Poems for love that never lasts.

Girl Poet

A collection of poems on the passion, privilege, and pain of being (or not quite being) a girl.

FRAMELESS

A collection of poems for the colors that make life vibrant, from their perspective, so we may share in what they might think and feel.

This One Has Pockets

Narrative poetry about a girl who is near giving up and the boy who tries to save her.

Core Series

Ava is the kind of girl who knows what's real and what isn't. Nothing in life is fair. Nothing is given freely. Nothing is painless. Every foster kid can attest to those truths, and Ava lives them every day. But when she meets a family of dragon shifters and is chosen to join them as a rider, her very notion of reality is shaken. She doesn't believe she can let her guard down. She doesn't think she can let them in—especially not the reckless, kind-eyed Cale. To say yes to him means he would be hers—her dragon and her companion—for life. But what if Ava has no life left to give?

The System Series

1 + 1 = Dead. That's the only math that adds up when you're in the System. Everywhere Nick turns, he's surrounded by the inevitability of his own demise at the hands of the people who stole his life from him. That is, until those hands deliver the bleeding, feisty, eye-rolling Nessa Parker. Tasked with keeping his new partner alive, Nick must face all the ways he's died and all the things
he's forgotten.

Nessa might as well give up. The moment she gets into that car, the moment she lays her hazel eyes on her new partner, her end begins. It doesn't matter that Nick Masters can slip through time by computing mathematical algorithms in his mind. It doesn't matter how dark and handsome and irre-sistibly cold he is. Nessa has to defeat her own shadows. Together and alone, Nick and Nessa make sense of their senseless fates and fight for the courage to change it all. Even if it means the System wins and they end up...well...dead.

Contact Teshelle Combs

Instagram @TeshelleCombs

Email: teshellecombs@gmail.com

Acknowledgments

Thank you to the people who stay. Nate, it has been
10 years of marrying the best human every day.
You are ever-changing and never-leaving.